# YOUNG LEARNER'S BIBLE STORIES

**Written by**
**Carol Watson and Julie Ferris**

ALLIGATOR®
www.alligatorbooks.co.uk
The Alligator logo is a registered trade mark of Alligator Books Ltd.

© 2007 Alligator Books Limited

Published by
Alligator Books Limited
Gadd House, Arcadia Avenue
London N3 2JU

Printed in India

# CONTENTS

# The Bible lands

In the times of the Bible, the world was very different from how it is today. Many of the countries and cities we know now didn't exist, or had different names. This map shows how the world was then. The map on page 46-47 shows what Bible lands are like today.

The mighty Roman Empire spread across many Bible lands in New Testament times (see page 28).

Olive oil lamps were used for lighting. People also used olive oil for cooking, cleaning and medicine.

The Ancient Greeks conquered many countries. They spread the Greek language and way of life to the Bible lands.

*Great Sea (Old Testament)*
*Mediterranean Sea (New Testament)*

The Ancient Egyptians were very powerful in Old Testament times (see page 14). Their kings were called pharaohs, and they were buried in huge stone pyramids by the Nile River.

MACEDON

Thessalonica

Corinth

GREECE

CRE

ITALY

SICILY

• Rome

## Houses

Most Bible lands were hot places, so homes were built of stone or mud brick to keep out the heat. Houses had flat roofs and small windows. Inside the house it was cool and shady.

Camels carried people and goods for long distances across the desert. They can live on poor food and go without water for several days.

A working man wore a white, knee-length tunic. He tucked this into his belt when he worked.

## Clothing

People wore long, flowing robes to keep cool. To protect their heads from the sun, they wore a turban, a piece of cloth held on with a cord.

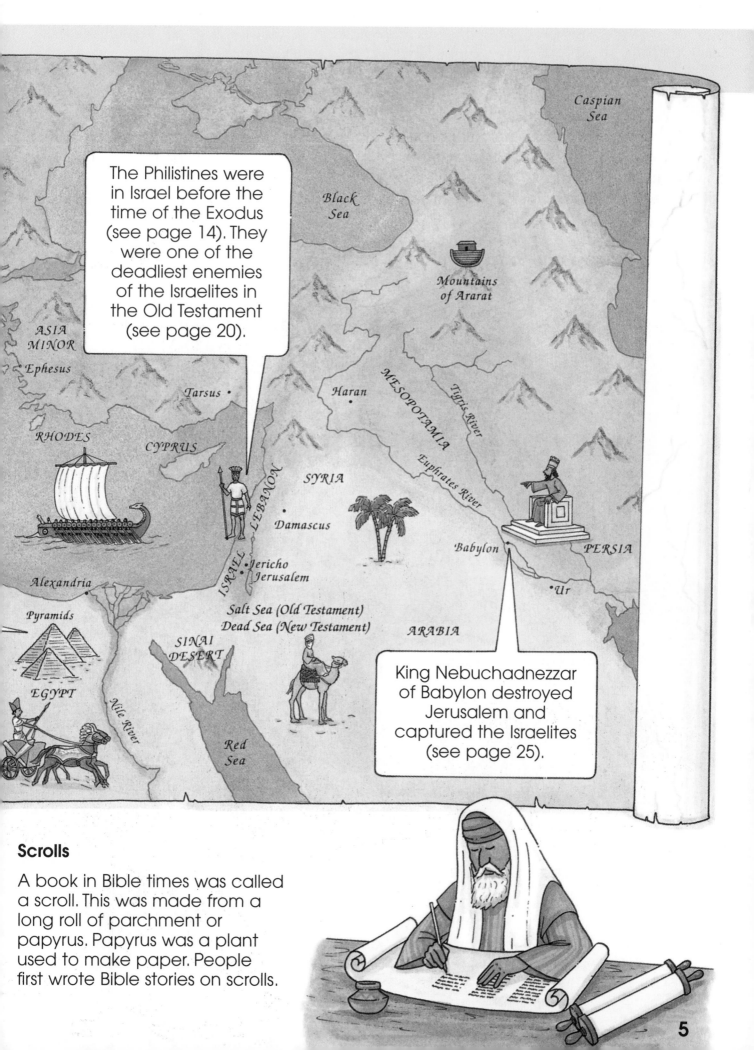

The Philistines were in Israel before the time of the Exodus (see page 14). They were one of the deadliest enemies of the Israelites in the Old Testament (see page 20).

Caspian Sea

Black Sea

Mountains of Ararat

ASIA MINOR

Ephesus

Tarsus •

Haran

MESOPOTAMIA

Tigris River

RHODES

CYPRUS

SYRIA

Euphrates River

Damascus

Babylon

PERSIA

ISRAEL   LEBANON

Jericho
Jerusalem

•Ur

Alexandria

Salt Sea (Old Testament)
Dead Sea (New Testament)

ARABIA

Pyramids

SINAI
DESERT

King Nebuchadnezzar of Babylon destroyed Jerusalem and captured the Israelites (see page 25).

EGYPT

Nile River

Red Sea

## Scrolls

A book in Bible times was called a scroll. This was made from a long roll of parchment or papyrus. Papyrus was a plant used to make paper. People first wrote Bible stories on scrolls.

# Why did Noah build an ark?

The Old Testament section of the Bible tells us that at the beginning of time God created the world, as well as the animals and birds, trees and flowers, rivers and seas. Everything that he made was wonderful. Next he created a man and a woman, called Adam and Eve, to enjoy this beautiful world.

## The Garden of Eden

Adam and Eve lived happily in the Garden of Eden. In the middle of the garden were two special trees. One was called the Tree of Life. The other was called the Tree of the Knowledge of Good and Evil. God told Adam that he was not allowed to eat the fruit from this tree.

## The serpent

The serpent persuaded Eve to eat some fruit from the forbidden tree. Then Eve tempted Adam to eat the fruit, too. God was angry. He cursed the serpent and sent Adam and Eve out of the Garden of Eden.

## The world outside the Garden of Eden

From then on, men and women had to work hard. They could no longer eat the fruit from the Tree of Life and live forever. They also knew the difference between good and evil, and a lot of them chose to lead wicked lives.

## Noah and the Flood

God grew more and more angry about people's wicked behaviour. Finally, he decided to kill everyone in a flood. However, there was one good man called Noah. God warned Noah about the flood and told him to build a huge boat, called an ark. Noah took two of every creature onto the ark with his family. Then it rained for forty days and nights, and water flooded the Earth. Everything was destroyed apart from the ark. After many months, the flood went down until the ark settled on the mountains of Ararat.

## God's promise

God promised Noah that he would never flood the Earth again. He called this agreement his 'covenant', and put a rainbow in the sky to remind people of his promise.

## Noah's sons

Noah's sons, Shem, Ham and Japheth, settled in different areas. They had children who grew up and had families of their own. These people were Noah's descendants.

# Who was Abraham?

One of Noah's descendants was a man called Terah, who lived with his family in Ur, Mesopotamia. The story of the nation of Israel begins with Terah's son, Abraham.

> Leave your country, your people and your father's household and go to the land of Canaan.

### God calls Abraham

As an old man, Terah left Ur with his family and set out for Canaan. He never reached Canaan, but instead settled down at Haran where he died. One day God spoke to Abraham, Terah's son, and told him to go to Canaan.

### Abraham obeys God

Abraham did what God asked. He left Haran and took his wife, Sarah, his nephew, Lot, his flocks, herds and all his belongings to Canaan.

### Altars to God

At Shechem and Bethel in Canaan, Abraham built altars and prayed to God. God told Abraham that he was going to give the land of Canaan to Abraham's children.

## The Negev Desert

Abraham then travelled down to the Negev Desert where there was grazing land for his animals. There wasn't enough food in the desert, so he went to Egypt for a while, later returning to the desert.

## Abraham and Lot part

After a time the flocks belonging to Abraham and Lot grew so large that there wasn't enough grazing land for them all to stay together. Lot moved to the Jordan Valley, while Abraham stayed in the hill country near Bethel and Ai.

Tigris River

MESOPOTAMIA

Euphrates River

Babylon

Ur

Shechem

Bethel

Ai

Jordan River

Salt Sea

Terah's journey

Abraham's journey

Lot's journey

## Nomads

Most people live in permanent homes. Nomads are people who move around the countryside taking their homes with them or building new ones wherever they stop. Abraham and his family were nomads. They travelled from place to place to find grazing land for their flocks of cattle, sheep and goats. Their animals provided them with meat to eat and milk to drink.

# How did God test Abraham?

For a long time Abraham and Sarah had no children. Then God blessed Sarah, and when she was quite old, she had a son, called Isaac.

Abraham, do not kill Isaac. Now I know that you are obedient to me. I will bless you. You will have as many descendants as there are stars in the sky.

## God tests Abraham

Isaac was very precious to Abraham. God tested Abraham's obedience by asking him to sacrifice Isaac. So Abraham took Isaac to a deserted place, but just as he was about to kill his son, God spoke to him.

## Sacrifices

To make a 'sacrifice' means to give up something that is precious to you. In Bible times people killed animals and offered them to God as a sacrifice. They did this to thank God or please him.

## Isaac and Rebekah

When Isaac grew up, he married a beautiful woman called Rebekah. She came from the land where Abraham had been born. Isaac and Rebekah had twin sons, called Esau and Jacob.

## Esau and Jacob

Esau was the elder of the twins, so he was due to receive the birthright and blessing from their father, Isaac. Jacob was jealous of Esau, so with the help of his mother, he tricked Esau out of his birthright and blessing.

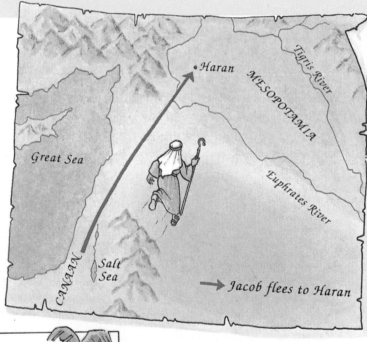

→ Jacob flees to Haran

### Birthright

The firstborn son always became head of the family after his father's death. He also inherited a double share of his father's possessions. This was called the 'birthright', and with it came his father's blessing for the future.

## Jacob leaves Canaan

Esau swore to kill Jacob once his father was dead. So Jacob fled to Haran to work for his uncle, who was called Laban.

→ Jacob returns to Canaan

## God blesses Jacob

After twenty years at Haran, Jacob owned huge flocks of sheep and herds of cattle and had two wives, called Rachel and Leah. They all returned to Canaan where Esau welcomed Jacob and forgave him for taking his birthright. It was then, that God blessed Jacob and gave him a new name, Israel.

# Who had a coat of many colours?

Jacob settled in Canaan with his wives and their families. He had many children, but his favourites were Joseph and his baby brother, Benjamin. They were the sons of Rachel, the wife Jacob loved the most.

## Joseph's coat

To show how much he loved him, Jacob gave Joseph a special coat of many colours. When Joseph's older brothers saw how much Jacob favoured Joseph, they were very jealous and hated him.

## Joseph is sold into slavery

One day Joseph visited his brothers, who were looking after the flocks of sheep at Dothan. When they saw Joseph coming, the brothers plotted to kill him.

## The spice trade

The spice trade was an important trade in Bible times. People used spices for food, incense and makeup. The trade route from Damascus, in Syria, to Egypt ran past Dothan, were Joseph's brothers sold him. The Ishmaelite spice traders were desert people, descended from Abraham.

However, some Ishmaelite spice traders passed by on their way to Egypt, so the brothers sold Joseph to the traders. They took Joseph to Egypt and sold him as a slave.

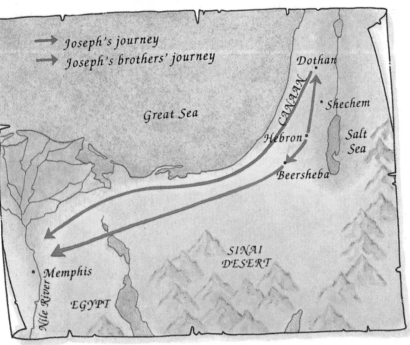

→ Joseph's journey
→ Joseph's brothers' journey

Dothan
Shechem
Great Sea
CANAAN
Hebron
Salt Sea
Beersheba
Memphis
Nile River
EGYPT
SINAI DESERT

## Pharaoh's dreams

For many years Joseph worked hard and was respected by his Egyptian master. God helped Joseph to understand people's dreams, so he was able to explain the strange dreams that were worrying the Pharaoh, who was the King of Egypt.

Your dreams mean that there will be seven years of good crops followed by seven years of famine. You should store grain for this time.

## The famine

The Pharaoh was so impressed with Joseph's advice that he put him in charge of all of Egypt. When the famine arrived, people came to Egypt from far and wide to buy grain. Joseph's brothers came from Canaan, but they didn't recognise Joseph in his smart Egyptian clothes.

## The Children of Israel

Finally, Joseph showed his brothers who he was and forgave them. They brought their old father, Jacob, and their families to live in Egypt. They were known as the Children of Israel.

## Ancient Egypt

The Nile River was the main source of life in Egypt. If the river was high, there was water for crops, but if the river was low, it meant that the crops died and people starved.

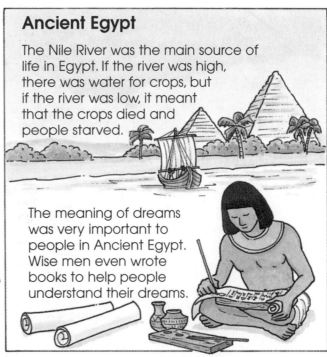

The meaning of dreams was very important to people in Ancient Egypt. Wise men even wrote books to help people understand their dreams.

# How did Moses escape from Egypt?

Hundreds of years later, the Children of Israel had grown into a large nation. The Pharaoh at that time was cruel and forced them to work as slaves. God chose Moses to lead the Israelites out of Egypt to begin the long journey back to Canaan. This journey was called the Exodus.

## Moses

Moses was born in Egypt. As a baby he was put in a basket on the Nile River. He was found and cared for by Pharaoh's daughter.

## God speaks to Moses

God spoke to Moses from a burning bush. He told him to ask Pharaoh to let the Israelites leave Egypt.

> I will set you free from your slavery. You will be my people, and I will be your God. I will give you a new land to live in, the land of Canaan.

Great Sea

Bitter Lakes

EGYPT

Nile River

→ The Exodus

## Disasters and plagues

Pharaoh would not let the Israelites leave, so God sent many disasters to Egypt. There were terrible diseases, storms and darkness, as well as plagues of flies, gnats, locusts and frogs. The water turned into blood.

## The worst disaster

Pharaoh still wouldn't listen, so God sent another disaster. One night the eldest son in every Egyptian family was killed, but God 'passed over' the Israelite families, and their sons survived. At last, Pharaoh told Moses to leave Egypt.

## The Passover

The Passover is a feast that the Jews still celebrate today. It reminds them of the time when God 'passed over' the houses of the Israelites when they were slaves in Egypt. During the Passover, Jews eat special bread that doesn't contain any yeast.

## The Israelites are chased

Moses led the Israelites to the edge of the sea where they camped. However, Pharaoh had changed his mind. His huge army was chasing the Israelites, who found themselves trapped between the Egyptian army and the sea.

Don't be afraid. God will keep you safe. He will fight for you.

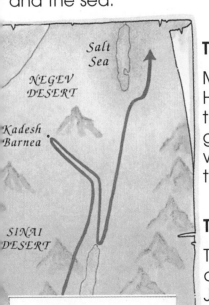

## The sea divides

Moses calmed the people. He stretched his arm out over the waves, and God sent a great wind, which parted the water, making a pathway through the sea.

## The Egyptians drown

The Israelites crossed the sea, and the Egyptian army chased after them. Just as the Israelites reached safe ground, God let the water pour back, and the huge Egyptian army was drowned beneath the waves. The Israelites were now free to begin their long journey through the desert.

In Bliblical times, the Red Sea may have extended further north than shown on our map, to the Bitter Lakes, which is where the crossing may have taken place.

# How many laws did God give Moses?

Moses led the Israelites into the desert. They soon forgot how God had rescued them from Egypt and began to grumble about the lack of food and water. God told Moses that he would give the Israelites meat and bread to eat.

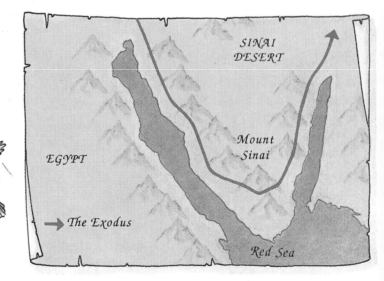

## Food from God

That night a flock of quails came down from the sky for the Israelites to eat. Then in the morning there was a layer of dew around the camp. When the dew had gone, thick frost-like flakes appeared on the ground. Moses told the people to collect this and eat it. They called it manna.

### Food in the desert

Quails are small brown birds. In winter they leave Europe and fly south. Their route takes them across the desert where the Israelites were at the time of the Exodus.

Manna was white and tasted like wafers made with honey. It was the Israelites' main food during their forty years spent wandering in the desert.

## Water from the rock

Moses led the Israelites on through the desert. As they grew short of water, they moaned. Moses asked God for help, so God told Moses to strike a rock with his walking stick. As he did so, water appeared from the rock for the people to drink.

## Mount Sinai

Months later the Israelites came to Mount Sinai. God told Moses that he would show his power to the Israelites. While Mount Sinai shook violently, they saw fire and lightning, and heard thunder and the loud blast of a trumpet. Then Moses climbed to the top of the mountain.

## The Ten Commandments

God told Moses that he would be the Israelites' God if they obeyed his laws. God wrote these laws on blocks of stone and gave them to Moses. The laws were called the Ten Commandments. They were rules about the correct way for the Israelites to live their lives as God's people.

## The tabernacle

God told Moses to build a large, movable tent to show the people that he was always with them. This tent was called the tabernacle. A special box, called an ark, was placed in it. This contained the Ten Commandments. The tabernacle was the holy place of God, and the ark was the holiest thing of all.

### Building the tabernacle

The Israelites handed over their finest possessions to make the tabernacle. These included fine linen, precious jewels and beautiful embroidery.

17

# Where was the Promised Land?

After wandering in the desert for forty years, Moses led the Children of Israel to the edge of the desert. They were close to Canaan, which was the Promised Land. Moses spoke to the Israelites and warned them not to forget God once they entered Canaan.

## Spies enter Canaan

Moses sent men into Canaan to check out the land. They reported back that it was a very good land, but there were large cities full of powerful people. The spies frightened the Israelites, who refused to enter Canaan. God was angry with them for not trusting that he would help them to defeat these people. As a punishment he made them wander in the desert for forty years. Moses died before they entered Canaan.

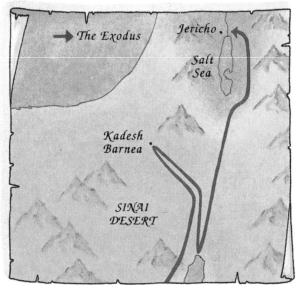

## Joshua and Jericho

After the death of Moses, God called Joshua, one of the Israelites, to lead his people into Canaan. The first city to be captured was Jericho. This had a large wall around it. God told Joshua to march his army around the city once a day for six days. At the front seven priests carried the ark (which contained God's written laws, as given to Mosses). On the seventh day they marched around seven times, with the priests blowing trumpets made of rams' horns. The people then shouted. The walls of Jericho came crashing down, and the Israelites took the city.

## Joshua's campaigns

After capturing Jericho, Joshua's army went on to capture the main cities all over Canaan. His first campaign began in the south, at Ai. The second campaign was in the north. Joshua divided the land that his army captured among the twelve Israelite tribes.

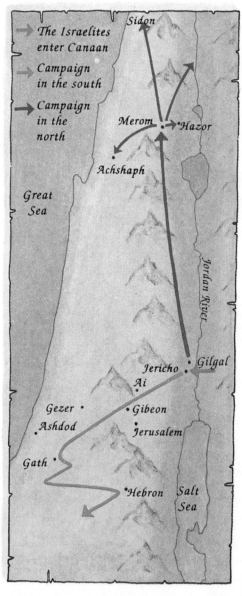

→ The Israelites enter Canaan

→ Campaign in the south

→ Campaign in the north

Sidon

Merom · →·Hazor

·Achshaph

Great Sea

Jordan River

Jericho· ·Gilgal
Ai

Gezer ·
Ashdod · · Gibeon

· Jerusalem

Gath ·

·Hebron    Salt Sea

# Who fought a giant?

For a long time after they had settled in Canaan, the tribes of Israel had many enemies. They fought battles against fierce armies, led by powerful kings. Their most deadly enemies were the Philistines. The people of Israel decided that it was time they had their own king to lead them against their enemies. This was because they had turned away from God, and no longer thought of him as their king.

→ *Battle with the Ammonites*

→ *Battle with the Philistines*

→ *Saul's last battle*

*Great Sea*

*CANAAN*

*NEGEV DESERT*

### Saul, the warrior king

God told Samuel to make Saul king of Israel. Samuel was a prophet, which meant he received messages from God. Saul led his army against the Ammonites and won a great victory. Then he defeated the Philistines. Saul won many battles, but he didn't always obey God. God was angry and decided that Saul should no longer be king.

### Saul and David

A shepherd boy called David was to be the next king. He went to live at Saul's court where he played music on his harp to soothe Saul's fits of depression. Saul did not know that David was the future king.

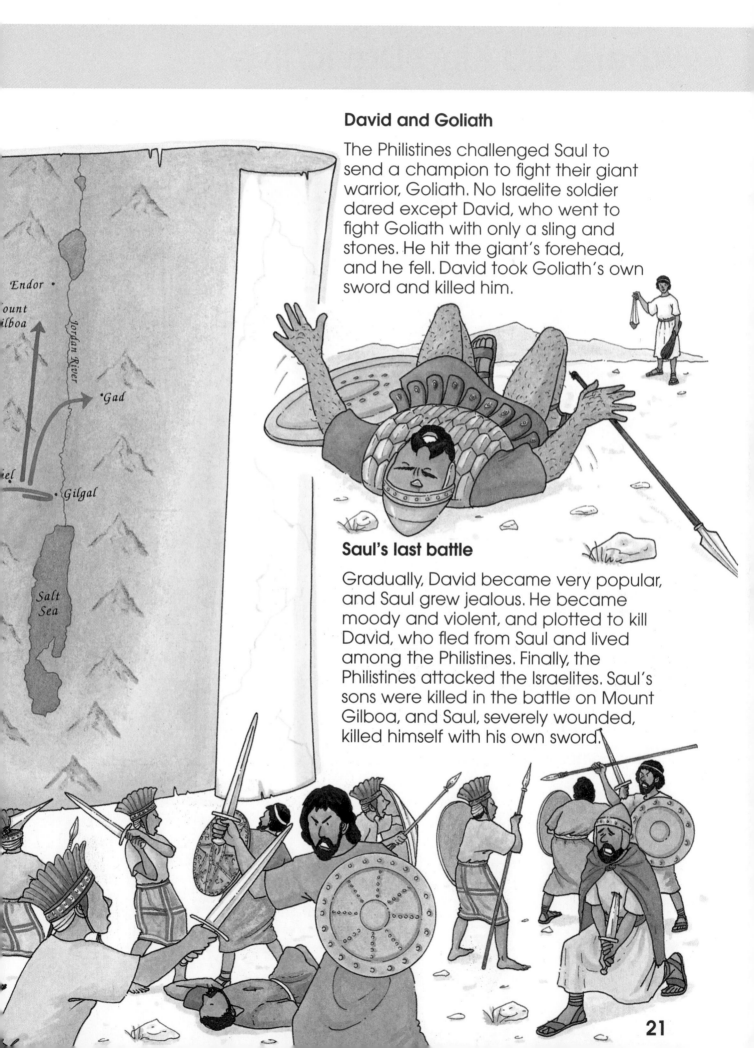

## David and Goliath

The Philistines challenged Saul to send a champion to fight their giant warrior, Goliath. No Israelite soldier dared except David, who went to fight Goliath with only a sling and stones. He hit the giant's forehead, and he fell. David took Goliath's own sword and killed him.

## Saul's last battle

Gradually, David became very popular, and Saul grew jealous. He became moody and violent, and plotted to kill David, who fled from Saul and lived among the Philistines. Finally, the Philistines attacked the Israelites. Saul's sons were killed in the battle on Mount Gilboa, and Saul, severely wounded, killed himself with his own sword.

Endor

Mount Gilboa

Jordan River

Gad

Gilgal

Salt Sea

21

# Where did King David live?

After Saul's death David became king of Israel. The first thing he did was to capture the fortress of Jerusalem and make it his capital. He called it 'The City of David'.

### David captures Jerusalem

The Jebusites lived in Jerusalem. They closed up the main entrance to the city and dug an underground tunnel to the water source outside the city walls. One of David's officers, called Jacob, found a way into the water tunnel. He and his men travelled up the tunnel and took the city by surprise.

### Jerusalem

David made Jerusalem into a city of great beauty and splendour. The work was continued by his son, Solomon. Today Jerusalem is still the capital of Israel where the government meets.

### The ark comes to Jerusalem

David made Jerusalem the holy city of Israel by taking the ark of the Lord there. The Israelites followed the ark and rejoiced. David sang praises to God and danced for joy. God promised David that his descendants would reign forever.

Praise the Lord!

## David conquers his enemies

Once David was king of Israel, the Philistines attacked him in full force. God told David to lead his army against them, and the Israelites had a great victory. David went on to defeat all his enemies, and he formed a large kingdom.

## Psalms of David

David wrote many poems, called psalms, to tell God how he was feeling. Some of them are happy and full of thanks and praise. Others show that David was sometimes angry or sad. David's psalms are collected together with other psalms in the Bible.

## David makes Solomon king

When David was a very old man, he promised his kingdom to his son Solomon. David told Solomon to obey God so that he would rule wisely and have a happy life.

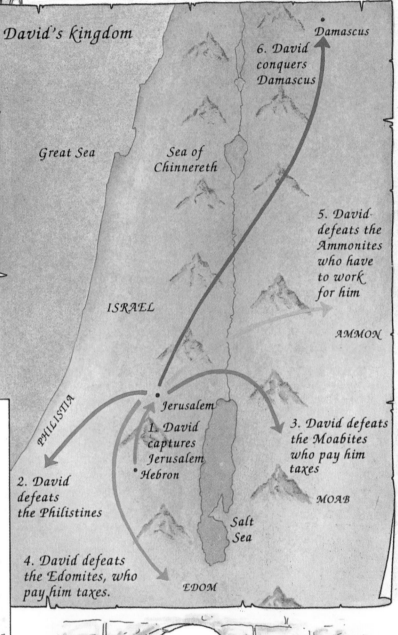

David's kingdom

Damascus

6. David conquers Damascus

Great Sea

Sea of Chinnereth

5. David defeats the Ammonites who have to work for him

ISRAEL

AMMON

PHILISTIA

Jerusalem

1. David captures Jerusalem

Hebron

3. David defeats the Moabites who pay him taxes

MOAB

2. David defeats the Philistines

Salt Sea

4. David defeats the Edomites, who pay him taxes.

EDOM

# What did Solomon build?

Solomon's reign as king was a time of peace and happiness for Israel. He was famous throughout the East for his great wealth and the beautiful buildings that he built in Jerusalem. Most of all, though, he was known for his great wisdom.

> I will give you wealth, as no king has had before or will again.

### God's gift of wisdom

When Solomon became king, God asked him what he wanted most. He asked for wisdom and knowledge, so that he would be a good king. God was pleased that Solomon hadn't asked for riches and other selfish things. He gave Solomon great wisdom and knowledge. He also gave him the riches he hadn't asked for.

### Solomon's wealth

Solomon was able to use his wisdom and knowledge to make clever business deals as well as wise decisions about governing Israel. He grew very rich and built a splendid palace.

## Solomon's trade

Egypt sells Solomon horses and chariots →

Solomon sells horses and chariots to the Syrians →

Solomon buys cedar wood for his temple from Lebanon →

Solomon builds a fleet of ships and trades his copper for gold, silver, ivory and jewels →

The Queen of Sheba visits Solomon →

### The temple

Solomon used his great wealth to build a temple for God. He ordered the finest materials from all over his kingdom and beyond. Thousands of cedar trees came from Lebanon, and the best quality stone was used. The walls inside the temple were covered with gold. After seven years the temple was finished. The people celebrated and worshipped God as the ark was brought to the temple. God was pleased with Solomon.

## Solomon's trade

Solomon was very successful in his trade with other countries. This increased his wealth even more. When the Queen of Sheba heard about Solomon's greatness, she visited him, bringing spices, gold and jewels.

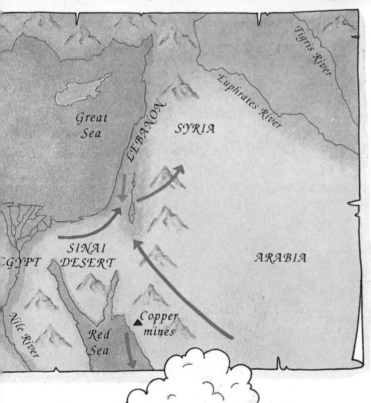

## Solomon's wives

Solomon had a thousand wives, who came from different kingdoms. They worshipped foreign gods and made the king turn away from the true God. God was very angry with Solomon because he had not honoured him and had not by abided the Ten Commandments. God warned Solomon that after his death his kingdom would be taken away from his family.

## After Solomon's reign

When Solomon died, fighting broke out, and the kingdom of Israel was split into two. Many years later King Nebuchadnezzar destroyed Jerusalem, captured its people, and took them to Babylon. Eventually, many of the Jewish people returned to rebuild their holy city.

# Who was swallowed by a whale?

God spoke to wise men called prophets. He told them to preach his word and to stop people worshipping false gods. God protected the prophets. He also gave some the gift to reveal the meaning of dreams.

## God calls on Jonah

God asked the prophet Jonah to travel to the city of Nineveh in Assyria. He wanted Jonah to preach to the people and change their wicked ways. But Jonah ignored what God told him to do. Instead, he boarded a ship and ran away.

## A stormy journey

The ship set sail and Jonah went below to rest. A terrible storm started. The crew was terrified. The sailors decided to draw lots to find out who was to blame for the disaster. They all wrote their names down and one was picked out. It was Jonah's name. Jonah realised he had disobeyed God. He told the crew to throw him overboard. As soon as Jonah sank beneath the waves, the sea grew calm.

## Jonah and the whale

God did not let Jonah drown. A great whale swallowed him. The whale carried Jonah to the shore and he travelled on to Nineveh. As God commanded, Jonah began to preach to the people.They realised they had been wrong and asked God's forgiveness for the way they behaved.

## Exile in Babylon

The armies of King Nebuchadnezzar of Babylon attacked Jerusalem. They captured many of its citizens and marched them to Babylon to work as slaves. The people of Judah who lived in exile in Babylon were called 'Jews' for short.

## Power of dreams

A young Jew called Daniel was chosen to work in Nebuchadnezzar's royal court. Daniel had the gift of understanding dreams. He became very rich and powerful and soon became a favourite of King Darius, but the other officials grew jealous. Every day Daniel prayed to God. When the officials saw this, they advised the king to pass a law saying that anyone who wants to ask for anything should only do so by consulting the king. If anyone made their request to another man or god, they would be thrown into a lion's den.

## In the lion's den

The officials spied on Daniel and saw that he was disobeying the law by praying to god. King Darius gave orders for Daniel to be thrown into a pit of lions. A huge stone was rolled over the entrance so there was no way of escape. The king was very unhappy about what the law had forced him to do. In the morning he rushed to the lion's den, but Daniel was still alive. The delighted king helped Daniel out of the den and ordered his people to worship Daniel's God.

# When did the Romans rule?

Four centuries later the Jewish people were once again under the control of a powerful enemy, the Romans. They had conquered Palestine (the Roman name for Canaan), and the Jews had to pay taxes to the Roman emperor. The Jews longed for freedom and wanted a saviour or a king, like David, to rescue them from their troubles.

## The Roman Empire

The Romans had a large army, which conquered many countries of the world. These became part of a huge empire that was ruled by the emperor in Rome, in Italy. In the years that they were powerful, there were many emperors. Augustus was the emperor at the time of Jesus's birth.

## Roman soldiers

Roman soldiers wore strong armour. They marched in large groups called legions, which were divided into smaller groups of fifty to a hundred men. Each group was led by a centurion. As well as fighting battles, the soldiers kept order in the cities ruled by the Romans. There were soldiers in Jerusalem whose job was to stop riots and carry out executions.

## King Herod the Great

The King of the Jews at this time was Herod. He was always trying to impress the Roman emperor and built a port for Augustus's ships at Caesarea. He also built palaces and an amphitheatre. Herod was allowed to rule over all of Palestine on Augustus's behalf.

## The new temple

King Herod was always worried that he was going to lose his power. He tried to please his people, the Jews, by building a large new temple in Jerusalem. Herod was king at the time of Jesus's birth.

## Roman developments

The Romans were famous for building straight roads all over their empire. You can still see some of these today. They also developed plumbing and central heating systems for houses.

# Where was Jesus born?

The New Testament section of the Bible tells us that a man called Joseph, who was a descendant of the great King David, lived in Nazareth, in Galilee. Joseph was a carpenter and worked hard for his living. He was happy because he was going to marry Mary.

> Don't be afraid, Mary. God is pleased with you. You are going to have a son who will be very special. You must call him Jesus. He will be God's promised king – the king who will reign forever.

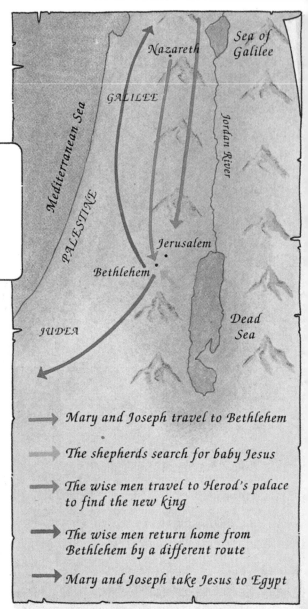

Mary and Joseph travel to Bethlehem

The shepherds search for baby Jesus

The wise men travel to Herod's palace to find the new king

The wise men return home from Bethlehem by a different route

Mary and Joseph take Jesus to Egypt

## Mary and the angel

One day when Mary was alone, a bright light filled the room, and a voice spoke to her. It was an angel, who told her that she was going to have a special baby who would be God's own son. Mary did not understand, but she promised to do what God wanted.

## The journey to Bethlehem

Mary and Joseph were married. Some months later Joseph had to travel to the town of Bethlehem, which was far away in Judea. Mary made the long journey with Joseph, even though it was almost time for her baby to be born.

## Jesus is born

There were so many visitors to Bethlehem that Mary and Joseph couldn't find anywhere to spend the night. At last, they found shelter in a stable. That night, among the animals, Mary's baby was born. As there was no cradle, she laid him in the manger to sleep.

## The shepherds

On the hillside outside Bethlehem, there were shepherds watching over their flocks of sheep. Suddenly, a bright light lit up the sky, and an angel spoke to them, telling them about the birth of Jesus, God's promised king. The shepherds searched until they found the baby in the stable. Then they knelt down and worshipped him.

## The wise men

Wise men from faraway lands in the East saw a bright new star shining in the sky. It was God's sign that a new king had been born. They told this to King Herod in Jerusalem, who decided to kill Jesus because he was frightened that Jesus would take over his throne. At last, the wise men found the house and gave Jesus expensive presents. However, they didn't tell King Herod where the baby was.

## King Herod's plot

King Herod was so frightened about the birth of Jesus that he ordered all the boys under two years old, in Bethlehem, to be killed. Mary and Joseph were warned about this in a dream. They escaped to Egypt where baby Jesus was safe.

31

# Who baptised Jesus?

Mary and Joseph returned from Egypt to live in Nazareth, where Jesus grew up. Jesus was waiting for the time when God would allow him to carry out his work. Jesus had a cousin, called John, who was a prophet. John told everyone they should live their lives the way God commanded and that God was sending someone special to them.

> You are my son, and I love you.

## Baptism

John the Baptist baptised people who wanted to obey God. Baptism involves covering a person with water. This was a symbol of washing away the things that the person had done wrong, so they could live their lives in a way that would please God.

## John the Baptist

When people heard John speak, some of them wanted to live better lives. John baptised them in the Jordan River. When it was time for Jesus to start God's work, he left Nazareth and was baptised by John. As Jesus came out of the water, God spoke to him saying that he loved him.

## Jesus calls his followers

After his baptism Jesus spent forty days in the desert where the devil tried to tempt him into using God's power in the wrong way. Then Jesus went to Galilee where he asked four fishermen, called Peter, Andrew, James and John, to follow him. They were the first followers of Jesus and were known as the disciples. Later there were eight more disciples.

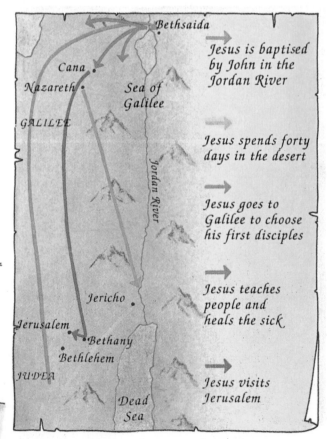

Bethsaida

Jesus is baptised by John in the Jordan River

Cana
Nazareth
Sea of Galilee
GALILEE

Jordan River

Jesus spends forty days in the desert

Jesus goes to Galilee to choose his first disciples

Jericho

Jesus teaches people and heals the sick

Jerusalem
Bethany
Bethlehem
JUDEA

Dead Sea

Jesus visits Jerusalem

## Jesus heals the sick

Jesus travelled to many places and talked to people about God. To make it easier for the crowds to understand what he was telling them, Jesus often used short stories, called parables, to explain something. Jesus also healed many sick people, some of whom had been ill for years. The news about Jesus spread far and wide, and large crowds gathered to hear him speak.

## Miracles

Jesus also showed God's power in ways other than healing. He calmed a fierce storm and walked on water. He changed water into wine at a wedding and fed five thousand people with only two fish and five loaves of bread. These were God's signs to people that his son was walking the Earth.

## Jesus comes to Jerusalem

When it was time to visit Jerusalem, Jesus entered the city on a donkey. The crowds welcomed him and cheered. They waved branches of palms and spread their cloaks on the road in front of him.

# What miracles did Jesus perform?

People travelled from far and wide to listen to Jesus preach. They also hoped to see him perform miracles. The crippled, lame, blind and deaf came to be healed by Jesus. These miracles showed people the true greatness of God's power and love.

### Healing the deaf and blind

Some people brought a deaf man to Jesus. Jesus gently placed his fingers in the man's ears. He looked up to heaven and prayed. Immediately the man was able to hear sounds all around him. Later a blind man was led to Jesus. Jesus carefully placed his hands on the man's eyes. 'Do you see anything?' Jesus asked him. Instead of darkness, the man could see bright lights, colours and shapes.

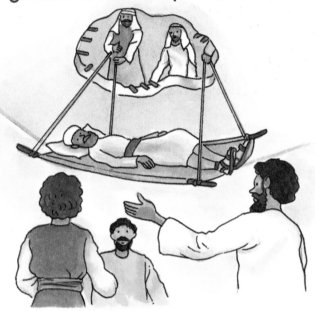

### Through the roof

Four men arrived at a house where Jesus was teaching. They were carrying a mat, on which lay their sick friend. The man was paralysed and could not move. The men could not get through the crowds. They carried their friend up steps to the flat mud roof and dug a hole. Then they lowered the sick man into the house. Jesus told the sick man to get up. The man stood up and walked through the crowds.

### Calming the storm

One day, Jesus had been healing people near the Sea of Galilee. When the sun went down, Jesus and his disciples climbed into a fishing boat and set sail. Jesus was very tired and fell asleep. A storm started. The disciples shook Jesus awake. Showing no fear, Jesus spoke to the wind and waves and said, 'Be still'. Just as suddenly as it started, the wind died down.

## Feeding the five thousand

Jesus was preaching to a crowd of five thousand. It grew very late and the people were feeling hungry. No one had any food except one young boy. All he had was five barley loaves and two small fish. Jesus told the disciples to divide the people into groups of fifty. He then divided the food among the people. The more Jesus shared out the bread and fish, the more bread and fish seemed to appear.

## Fish

Fish was an important food in Jesus's time. Small fish were dried and salted, eaten with bread. Or they could be cooked over an open fire and eaten fresh.

## Walking on water

One evening the disciples went out in a boat. Jesus stayed on the shore to pray. When he was finished he stepped onto the water and walked towards the disciples. In the moonlight, the disciples thought the figure was a ghost. Jesus told Peter, one of the disciples, to walk towards him. Peter got out of the boat and walked on the water. Suddenly he felt afraid and started to sink. Jesus reached out his hand and caught Peter. When they climbed into the boat, the disciples said to Jesus, 'You really are the Son of God'.

# What did Jesus teach?

Jesus taught people about God and how they should live their lives. He explained that they should love one another and God. He often used simple stories, called parables, to explain his teachings.

The Lord's Prayer

'Our Father in heaven,
hallowed be your name,
your kingdom come,
your will be done
on earth as it is in heaven.
Give us this day our daily bread.
Forgive us our sins
as we forgive those who sin against us.
And lead us not into temptation
but deliver us from evil.
For yours is the kingdom,
the power and the glory for ever,

Amen.

## Sermon on the Mount

One day, Jesus and his disciples taught a large crowd on a mountainside. Jesus explained that people should be kind and loving. He said you should treat your enemies as you would like to be treated yourself. Jesus advised rich people not to buy all sorts of expensive things that they did not need. Instead they should give their spare money to the poor.

## Saying prayers

As part of his Sermon on the Mount, Jesus told his followers how to pray to God. He explained that prayers should be simple and honest. Jesus taught the crowd a new prayer – the Lord's Prayer. The prayer praises God and asks him for the food we need to live. It also asks God to forgive any wrongdoing.

## The sower

Jesus often taught by telling people stories about things that happened in everyday life. One of these parables was about a farmer sowing seeds in the fields. As he scattered the seed, some fell on the path and was eaten by birds. Other seed fell on rocky places where it couldn't put down deep roots. Some seeds fell among thorns. When the plants grew, the thorns choked them. The seed that fell on good soil took root and grew strong.

## The meaning

Jesus explained that the farmer is the person who spreads God's message. The seed is the word of God. Some people are like the seed sown on the path. As soon as they hear God's word, the devil makes them forget all about it. Others are like the seed on rocky ground. As their belief is not deep-rooted, they soon give up on God. Those like the seed that falls among thorns hear God's message, but other desires take over. Those who are like the seed sown on good soil hear God's message and take it into their hearts.

## The Good Samaritan

Jesus taught that you should love your neighbour as yourself. He told a story to explain what he meant. A man was attacked by a gang of thieves. They beat him up and left him by the roadside. Several people passed by, but they did not stop. A Samaritan walked by. The Jews and Samaritans had long been enemies, but the Samaritan stopped to help. He tended the man's wounds and carried him to the nearest inn. Even though he was an enemy, he proved to be the best neighbour.

# Why was Jesus crucified?

In Jerusalem, Jesus continued his teaching. Each day crowds of people came to hear him speak outside the temple. The Jewish chief priests became angry because Jesus said he was the Son of God, and they didn't believe him. They thought of ways to kill him, but they were frightened of all the people who supported Jesus.

## The Last Supper

Jesus and his disciples gathered together to celebrate the feast of the Passover (for more details of the feast see page 14). Jesus told them that it would be the last meal he would eat with them, and that one of them was going to turn against him.

As Jesus gave out the bread and passed around the cup of wine, he told the disciples that the bread and wine were symbols of his body and blood. He asked them to remember him by eating bread and drinking wine together in the future.

## Jesus prays

During the night, Jesus went to a quiet garden at Gethsemane, so that he could pray. He knew what was going to happen to him, and he was feeling very nervous.

## Jesus is seized

Just after Jesus had prayed, a crowd of people appeared. One of the disciples, called Judas Iscariot, led the way. Jesus's enemies had paid Judas thirty silver coins to tell them where they could seize Jesus secretly. Some soldiers then took hold of him and led him away. Afterward, Judas realised what a terrible thing he had done, and he killed himself.

## Jesus is crucified

Jesus was sentenced to death by the Jewish high court and taken to the Roman governor, Pontius Pilate. The chief priests, among others, demanded that Jesus be crucified because he was the Son of God. They shouted so much that finally Pilate agreed. They took Jesus to a place called Golgotha and nailed him to a wooden cross. Before he died on the cross, Jesus asked God to forgive the people who had crucified him.

Father, forgive them.

## Jesus rises from the dead

After Jesus died, his body was put inside a cave. Three days later, visitors found that the stone had been moved and Jesus's body was gone! They saw an angel in the cave, who told them not to be afraid because Jesus had risen from the dead and was alive.

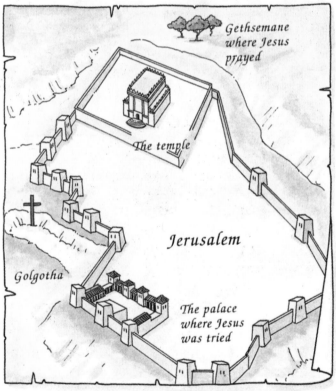

## The disciples see Jesus

Jesus appeared to the disciples as they were eating together. When they saw the marks of the nails in his hands and feet, they believed it was really Jesus. He told his disciples to go and tell people about God and to heal the sick, just as he had done.

# How did Christianity spread?

After Jesus had risen from the dead, he ate and talked with his disciples many times. He told them that God was going to give them the Holy Spirit. The word *spirit* means 'breath', so the Holy Spirit is the breath of God as Jesus is the Son of God. After Jesus had made this promise, he went up to join God in heaven. This is called the Ascension.

### Pentecost

Pentecost was the Jewish harvest festival when the Jews remembered God giving Moses the Ten Commandments on Mount Sinai. Today, at Pentecost, Christians remember when the Holy Spirit first came.

### The Holy Spirit

Not long after Jesus had left them, the disciples met in Jerusalem for the festival of Pentecost. As they prayed together, a sound like a strong wind suddenly filled the house, and what seemed like flames of fire appeared above their heads.

### Different languages

The disciples were filled with the Holy Spirit and began to speak languages that they had not known before. Jews from other countries who were also there were amazed as they heard their own language spoken. They listened to the disciples speaking about the wonderful things God had done, and asked one another how this could possibly happen.

Rome

ITALY

MACEDONIA

SICILY

GREECE

CRETE

Mediterranean Sea

Cyrene

→ After Pentecost many Christians return to their own countries and speak about Jesus

→ After Stephen's death some Christians leave Israel

## Peter preaches

After this, Peter preached to people in Jerusalem. He told them that God had raised Jesus from the dead. Thousands of people listened to Peter and believed what he said. They were baptised by the disciples and became Christians. When they returned to their own countries, they told people about Jesus.

## Christians

Christians are followers of Jesus Christ. They believe that people who follow Jesus are forgiven for all the wrong things they do. They also believe that they will be allowed to live forever with God after they have died.

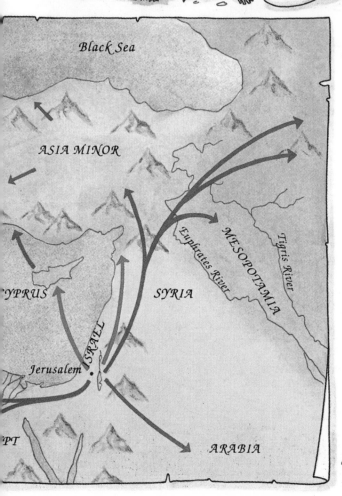

## Stephen, the martyr

The Jewish high priests looked for ways to stop people from speaking about Jesus. They seized a powerful Christian speaker called Stephen and wrongly accused him of speaking against God and Moses. Then Stephen's enemies killed him by throwing stones at him. Stephen became the first Christian martyr. A martyr is someone who suffers or dies for what he or she believes in.

# How did Saul become a Christian?

One of the people in charge of seizing Christians was a man called Saul. He had stood by and watched as Stephen was stoned to death. Saul was born in the Roman city of Tarsus, but he grew up and was educated in Jerusalem. Saul was very eager to wipe out people's belief in Jesus Christ. He even tracked down Christians who had fled from Jerusalem.

> Saul, Saul, why are you against me? I am Jesus.

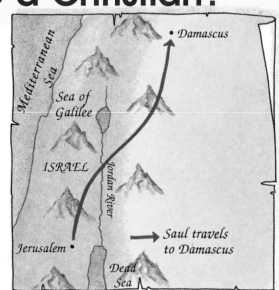

## The road to Damascus

One day Saul was travelling to Damascas to seize some Christians. Suddenly, as he neared the city, a bright light from heaven flashed around him, and he heard a voice calling to him.

## Saul is baptised

The light blinded Saul, and he had to be lead into Damascus. A Christian called Ananias visited him. Ananias prayed for Saul, and his eyes were healed so that he could see again. Then Saul was baptised and became a Christian. Later he changed his name to the Roman name Paul.

## Damascus

Damascus is one of the oldest cities in the world. In New Testament times many Christians lived there. It is now the capital of Syria.

42

## Paul escapes

The Jews in Damascus were shocked when Paul became a Christian, and they plotted to kill him. However, other Christians helped him to escape from the city by lowering him down the outside of the city wall in a basket.

## Paul's travels

Paul went to Jerusalem where he met Peter and other disciples. Again he had to escape from angry Jews. Paul went to Caesarea, and then on to his home city of Tarsus. He stayed there for ten years, speaking about Jesus. Then a disciple called Barnabas went with Paul to Antioch where they taught people about Jesus.

### Apostle to the Gentiles

The first disciples chosen by Jesus became known as the Apostles. Jesus and his disciples had travelled all over Israel, but Paul took the message of Jesus to people who were not Jews. The Jews call non-Jewish people 'Gentiles', so Paul became known as the 'Apostle to the Gentiles'.

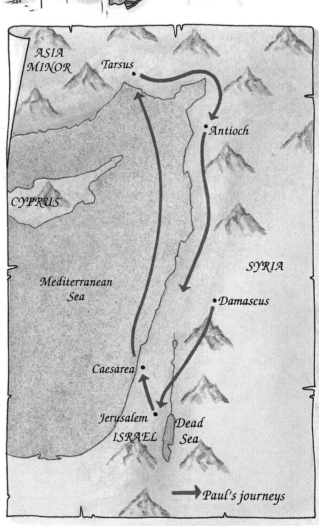

Paul's journeys

## Paul returns to Jerusalem

Paul returned to Jerusalem and met the Christian leaders there. In spite of some disagreement, the leaders agreed that Paul should preach to both Jews and Gentiles.

# What countries did Paul visit?

For many years Paul travelled all over the lands around the Mediterranean. He spoke about Jesus Christ to people from many different nations. He and other disciples went through all kinds of danger in order to teach people and heal the sick.

## Paul's journeys

Paul went on three main journeys. On the first journey he visited Cyprus, and his second and third journeys took him through Asia Minor to Greece. Finally, Paul returned to Jerusalem.

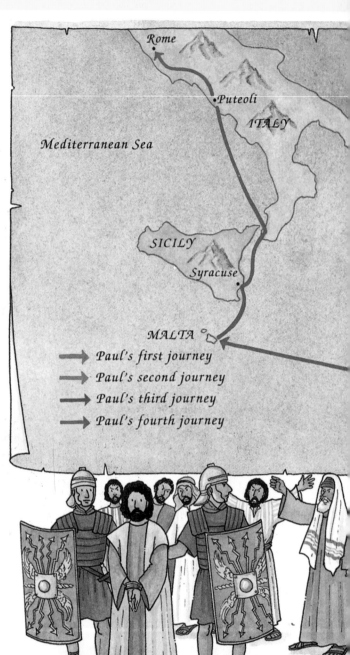

Paul's first journey
Paul's second journey
Paul's third journey
Paul's fourth journey

## Trouble in Jerusalem

As Paul was speaking about Jesus in Jerusalem, angry Jews tried to kill him. He was rescued by Roman soldiers and sent to the Roman governor in Caesarea, to be tried.

## Paul goes to Rome

After two years in prison, Paul appealed to the Roman emperor. Under armed guard, he was put on a ship heading for Rome. During the journey he travelled on three different ships. One of these was a cargo ship carrying grain to Rome.

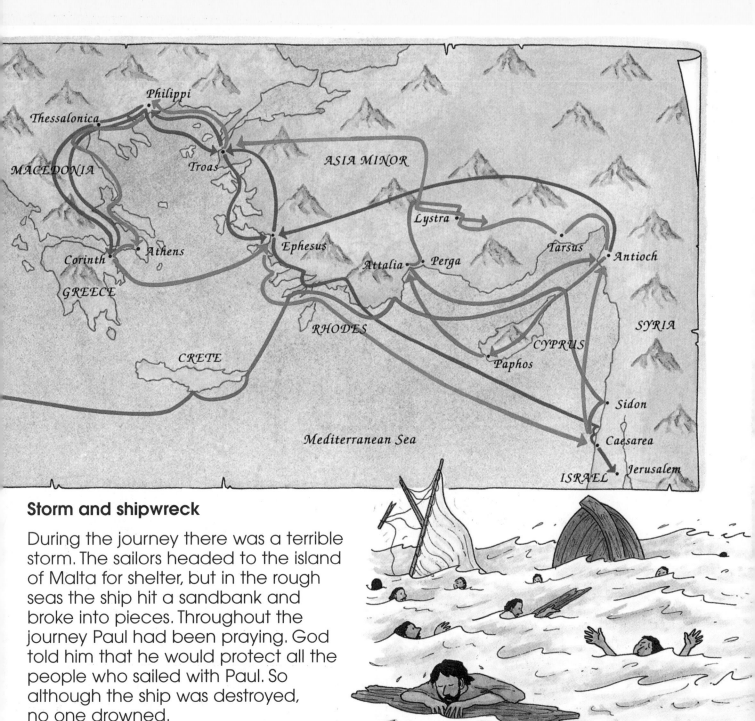

## Storm and shipwreck

During the journey there was a terrible storm. The sailors headed to the island of Malta for shelter, but in the rough seas the ship hit a sandbank and broke into pieces. Throughout the journey Paul had been praying. God told him that he would protect all the people who sailed with Paul. So although the ship was destroyed, no one drowned.

## Paul in Rome

Months later Paul reached Rome. For two years he was allowed to live in his own house with soldiers guarding him. He spoke about Jesus Christ to everyone who came near him.

### Paul's letters

Paul wrote long letters to the various groups of Christians he had visited on his travels. In these letters Paul wrote down details of how Christians should try to live their lives. Paul's letters are in the Bible and are read by Christians today.

# What are the Bible lands like today?

The bible lands have belonged to many different races of people since Biblical times. This map shows you the countries and cities that you will find there now.

Many countries have oil under the ground. This is pumped to the surface at oil wells and shipped to all parts of the world in huge oil tankers.

Citrus fruits, figs, dates and olives from Israel are sent all over the world.

Office blocks, hotels and other tall, modern buildings now tower above the remains of many old cities.

St Peter's Church in Rome is the biggest Christian church in the world.

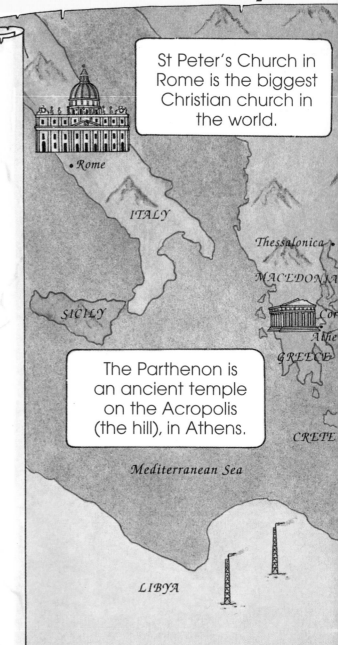

- Rome

ITALY

Thessalonica

MACEDONIA

SICILY

Cor

Athe

GREECE

The Parthenon is an ancient temple on the Acropolis (the hill), in Athens.

CRETE

Mediterranean Sea

LIBYA

Many tourists go to Israel, the Holy Land, to see where Jesus lived. People also visit the ruins of ancient buildings in other countries.

AFRICA

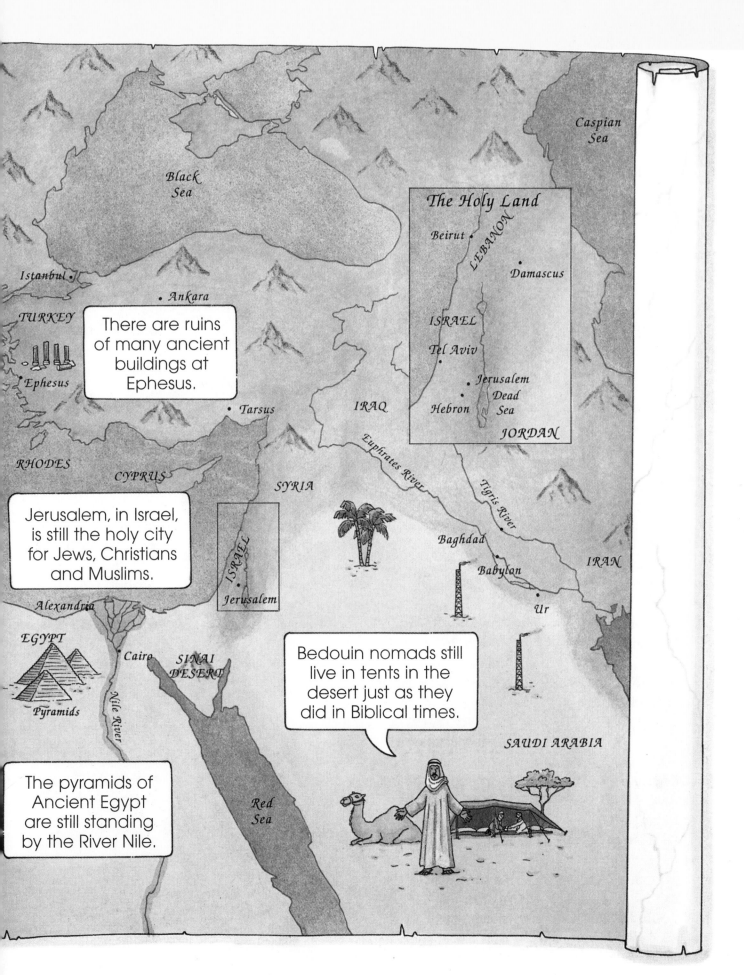

There are ruins of many ancient buildings at Ephesus.

Jerusalem, in Israel, is still the holy city for Jews, Christians and Muslims.

Bedouin nomads still live in tents in the desert just as they did in Biblical times.

The pyramids of Ancient Egypt are still standing by the River Nile.

Black Sea

Caspian Sea

The Holy Land

Beirut • LEBANON

• Damascus

ISRAEL

Tel Aviv •

• Jerusalem
Dead Sea

Hebron •

JORDAN

Istanbul •

• Ankara

TURKEY

Ephesus •

• Tarsus

IRAQ

RHODES

CYPRUS

SYRIA

ISRAEL

Jerusalem •

Euphrates River

Tigris River

Baghdad •

Babylon •

IRAN

Ur •

Alexandria

EGYPT

Cairo •

SINAI DESERT

Nile River

Pyramids

Red Sea

SAUDI ARABIA

# Index